MARCEL PEREZ

THE INTERNATIONAL MIRTH-MAKER

BY

STEVE
MASSA

Cover design by Marlene Weisman-Abadi
Editing and layout by Ben Model

image on front cover : EYE Filmmuseum, Netherlands,
Desmet Collection

A publication of Undercrank Productions.
www.undercrankproductions.com

Marcel Perez: The International Mirth-Maker
Copyright © 2015 Steve Massa.

ISBN: 1503038912
ISBN-13: : 978-1503038912

DEDICATION

Dedicated to the many overlooked men and women of silent comedy whose artistry and hard work, in front of and behind the camera, have been forgotten due to the passage of time and the loss of their films.

EDITOR'S NOTE

We have endeavored to include as many of the available images from the films of Marcel Perez in this book as possible. This has been done, especially in the case of Perez's American comedies, to aid in the locating or identification of lost films.

INTRODUCTION

Perhaps the best silent comedian whom no one's ever heard of is Marcel Perez. Part of the very first generation of screen clowns, his career began in 1900 and flourished until 1928. During that time he helped create the ground rules for the genre in Europe and continued to refine the basics in America. An international favorite, Perez was, along with Max Linder, one of the few direct links between European and American silent Comedy, and made over 200 starring shorts. The obscurity that he's fallen into is a combination of the passage of time, the scarcity of his surviving work, and the gypsy-like way he traveled through early film comedy – constantly re-naming himself and his screen character.

It was almost fifteen years ago, in 2000, that I first came across one of his films during a screening of unidentified silent comedy shorts at the Museum of Modern Art. Listed as *[Unidentified Tweedy Comedy. 1916]* (a.k.a. *Vsudybl Si Vypusci Cizi Zenu* since it had turned up in Czechoslovakia), it was a farce about a guy who borrows a buddy's wife to trick a rich uncle into thinking that he's married and settled down. Although a standard comedy plot, I was struck by the lead comedian's originality and goofy persona, and very amused by the way he couldn't resist hitting on the friend's wife despite the seriousness of the situation with his uncle.

1

The only information that MoMA had was that the star was Marcel Perez, and that the film was made by the Eagle Film Company in 1916. Surprised that I had never heard of him before, I got completely hooked a couple of months later when I saw another – *Vsudy Byl A Vse* (or *He's Some Hero*). This one was a spoof of cliffhanger serials full of non-stop cartoony and surreal gags. Thanks to Perez's antic imagination, not to mention the unusual Florida locations, these two shorts didn't look anything like the standard Hollywood comedy shorts and had a unique mindset that was all their own.

On looking for information on Marcel Perez in the basic film comedy texts I immediately came up short – his name was nowhere to be found. Checking with fellow silent comedy mavens such as Sam Gill and Cole Johnson I got bits of info – "His character was Tweedledum, "In Europe he worked as Marcel Fabre," and "After he came to the U.S. he disappeared." Finally I found a bare bones entry in David Robinson's 1969 book *The Great Funnies*:

> As 'Robinet' Marcel Fabre had equal success before going to America to star in a series of Vim Comedies. After losing his arm in an accident, he was obliged to become a gag-man at Universal.

Although not entirely correct, this crystalized his basic story and gave me a sound base to start searching. Armed with these few tidbits I practically took up residence at the New York Public Library for the Performing Arts at Lincoln Center with their microfilm reels of film journals like *Moving Picture World* and *Motion Picture News*, going through them page by page for items on the elusive Mr. Perez. Starting in 1916, with his work for Eagle I found that the films I had seen were *Lend Me Your Wife* (November 13, 1916) and *Some Hero* (October 23, 1916). Continuing on, I worked my way into the 1920s, and then backtracked to his work before he came to America, and I realized I had seen one of his Italian comedies, *Amor Pedestre* (1914). Eventually I was able to chart that Marcel Fabre, Fernandez Perez, and Marcel Perez were all the same person, and that Robinet, Tweedledum, Bungles, Twede-Dan, and Tweedy were all different monikers for his on-screen persona.

At the same time, I worked on tracking down as many of his films as possible. More were found, and have been included on the *Marcel Perez Collection* DVD, in the collections of the Library of Congress and the EYE Filmmuseum, Netherlands. I was able to view the comedies at Library of Congress thanks to the helpful and dedicated staff at their Motion Picture Reading Room in Washington, DC. I had recently begun consulting with EYE Filmmuseum, helping to identify the many unidentified American silent comedies they had, and they generously provided Perez screeners and information (later more of their Robinet shorts were used in the 2012 "Euro-Clowns" edition of our MoMA series *Cruel and Unusual Comedy*, selected by Ron Magliozzi, Ben Model, and myself from EYE's incredible Desmet Collection). Everything I gathered at the time was put into the article *Tweedy's Tangled Tale* for the #6 issue of *Slapstick!* magazine in 2002. Almost immediately, more info and films began resurfacing, so that piece was updated a few years later and included as a chapter in my 2013 book *Lame Brains and Lunatics: The Good, The Bad, and The Forgotten of Silent Comedy*. After the book's publication, even more pertinent items have come to light, and these have been incorporated in this latest incarnation.

Before moving on to Mr. Perez's saga I'd first like to give special thanks to Ben Ohmart of Bear Manor Media for allowing me to update and revise my Perez chapter and filmography from *Lame Brains and Lunatics*. Over the last fifteen years the following friends and colleagues have gone beyond the call of duty in their sharing of and helping to track down information, photos, and films on this enigmatic figure – Robert S. Birchard, Eileen Bowser, Lisa Bradberry, Serge Bromberg, Jared Case, David Denton, Sam Gill, Rosemary Haine, Michael J. Hayde, Chad Hunter, Cole Johnson, Giovanni Lasi, Ron Magliozzi, Mike Mashon, Madeline Matz, Jon Mirsalis, Ben Model, Rachel Parker, James Perez, Juanita Perez, Leenke Ripmeester, David Robinson, Elif Rongen-Kaynakci, Steve Rydzewski, Uli Ruedel, Charles Silver, Zoran Sinobad, Liz Stanley, Rob Stone, Brent Walker, and Barbara Whitehead, not to mention the conservation and preservation staffs of the Library of Congress, EYE Filmmuseum, Netherlands, the Museum of Modern Art, and George Eastman House.

MARCEL PEREZ:
THE INTERNATIONAL MIRTH-MAKER

Perez, Manuel Fernandez, comedian, Eagle Film; b. Madrid, Spain, 1885; educ., France; screen career at age 15 with Ambrosio Film in Italy, later with Pathé for 2 yrs., Eclipse for 3 yrs. And Éclair for 4 yrs; now Eagle ("Tweedledum" in "Tweedledum and Tweedledee" comedies). Recreations, swims, paints, etc.; has written scenarios and done his own directing. Hght. 5 ft; wght. 125; black hair and eyes. Studio address. Eagle Film Co., Jacksonville, Fla.

Marcel Perez's birth, like the majority of his life and work, is the subject of conflicting information. In common with his fellow obscure comic Charley Bowers, Perez seemed to have been fond of tall tales, and took the opportunity to give multiple choices whenever possible for the basic facts of his story. Instead of picking a, b, or c, I've decided to present all of the above and let the reader decide what seems the most likely.

The above bio is a standard one from the October 21, 1916 *Motion Picture News Studio Directory*, and says that Perez was born in Madrid. His death certificate however gives his birth place as Africa, and since that info came from his widow it's possible that he was born in one of Africa's Spanish colonies. His date of birth is also a bit elastic as well – sometimes 1884, 1885, or 1888. Spending his early years in Paris, he grew up on stage, clowning in circuses and music halls before entering films around 1900. Again the bio seems turned around as he didn't join Ambrosio until 1910 and his first movie work appears to have been for Pathé. At the moment, his earliest known appearance is in the 1904 Pathé comedy *Les Devaliseurs Nocturnes* (a.k.a *Burglars at Work*). Released in America in 1908 as *Nocturnal Thieves*, the plot has Perez and a cohort breaking into a miser's house, and the film makes charming use of silhouettes double-exposed over other footage to put a fresh comic spin on a familiar burglar story.

Also working for Éclair, he had his first big hit with the Eclipse Company in 1907. *The Short-Sighted Cyclist* stars Perez as a bicycle messenger who loses his glasses and runs into workmen, horse-carts, shop displays, and everything else in his path before finally driving off a bridge into the river. Thanks to its popularity and the number of prints struck, it's one of the earliest surviving Eclipse films. Another survivor from his early days in France is the 1910 Gaumont film *Le Police l'an 2000 (Police in the Year 2000)*, about a future police force who travel in a dirigible, capturing wrongdoers with long hooks. Perez portrays an apprehended safecracker and spends most of his screen time trying to grab the camera's attention.

At this time European comedies were booming and stars had emerged such as Andre Deed, Max Linder, Charles Prince, and Ferdinando Guillame. Thanks to his popularity since *The Short-Sighted Cyclist*, Perez got his own starring series as Robinet in numerous one-reelers for the Ambrosio Company of Italy. Based in Turin, Ambrosio was founded in 1906 by Arturo Ambrosio and specialized in historical dramas and epics. They also had a line of comedies that included Ernesto Vasar starring as "Fricot" and Gigetta Morano in her own "Gigetta" shorts (both would appear on occasion with Perez). In 1910 Perez joined the fun under the name Marcel Fabre and was an instant success as the character Robinet, an anarchic everyman who seemed to live to turn society's bourgeois conventions upside-down and provide his own surreal spin to reality.

Many of the surviving comedies center around Robinet's obsessions and single-minded determination to carry them out, which always leads to absurd extremes and his landing in hot water. In *L'Abito Bianco di Robinet* (*Robinet's White Suit*, 1911) he decides to hit the town in his new all-white suit, but of course he quickly comes into conflict with the blackening industrial city landscape. *Robinet Inamorato di una Chanteuse* (*Robinet in Love with a Cabaret Singer*, 1911) has his passion for the title character cause him to disrupt an entire vaudeville show and even stalk her at home. Slightly different is *Robinet Troppo Amato due sua Moglie* (*Robinet is Too Much Much by his Wife*, 1912), where this time the obsession is his wife's for him, driving him crazy with her over-devoted attentions. Trying to escape her fussing, he meets a cute girl in the park and manages to lock wifey in a closet so he can spend the afternoon with his new sweetie.

Madamigella Robinet (*Madamoiselle Robinet*, 1912) explores sexual politics when, to escape from his lover's husband, he dresses in her clothes and pretends to be a visiting friend. Not only does the husband hit on him, but after making his escape he has to walk home in drag and is chased by the majority of the older men in town. Mistaken obsession is the whole point of *Robinet e Geloso* (*Robinet is Jealous*, 1914) where his suspicion that Robinette is cheating on him causes him to follow her to a building to catch her in the act. Unfortunately for him, he keeps bursting into the wrong apartments and is continually beaten and pummeled until he finds that his wife had only commissioned an artist to sculpt a bust of him.

Actress Nilde Baracchi had joined him in 1911 as his love interest Robinette, and would work with him for many years. Perez's best known film from his Ambrosio days is *Amor Pedestre* (*Love Afoot*, 1914), which showcases his sophistication and ingenuity as a director with a clever version of a love triangle soap opera that is performed entirely by the actors' feet. At the same time as his Robinet shorts were in production, Perez filmed a serialized adaptation of Ferdinand Robida's novel *Le Avventure Straordinarissme di Saturnino Farrandola (The Extraordinary Adventures of Saturnino Farandola,* 1914) which was a parody of the Jules Verne type of adventure epics.

Told in four episodes, Perez tones down his Robinet persona to play the young hero who (despite being raised by monkeys on a tropical island) is valiant and ever-resourceful in all kinds of fantastic scrapes. The locations include the bottom of the ocean, a mad scientist's laboratory, ancient Asia, an America with hostile Indians, and war dirigibles in the sky. Only existing today in a seventy-eight minute condensation, there are continuity gaps and a bit too much action crammed together, but it's a superb and breathtakingly beautiful film where director Perez keeps his tongue firmly in his cheek. While the scope of the production and sets match many of the epic German silents from the teens and twenties, *Farandola* always remains charming and funny.

Unique publicity card for the Robinet series with Perez, Baracchi, and their supporting players. Ernesto Vasar is hanging fourth from the left. *Museo Nazionale del Cinema*

Perez dreaming of being on horseback from *Robinet Vuol Fare il Jockey* (*Robinet Wants to be a Jockey*, 1910). *Museo Nazionale del Cinema*

One of the many crashes from *Robinet Chauffeur Miope* (*Robinet the Near-Sighted Chauffeur*, 1914). *Museo Nazionale del Cinema*

Perez and friend from *Robinet Perde e Guadagna* (*Robinet Lost and Won*, 1914). This unknown actress previously starred in the French *Cunegonde* series in 1911 to 1913 for the Lux Company. *Museo Nazionale del Cinema.*

Perez has his doubts about Robinette (Nilde Baracchi) in *Robinet e Geloso* (*Robinet is Jealous*, 1914). *Museo Nazionale del Cinema.*

The bust seen in *Robinet e Geloso* (1914) was not merely a prop, it was a sculpture of Perez by the famed Italian sculptor Cezare Zocchi. The circumstances surrounding the making of the bust are not known, although Zocchi signed it 1912 on the bottom. Zocchi's son, also Cesare Zocchi, was an actor and director at Ambrosio, and he plays two roles in the film: a boxer and a sculptor. Perez brought the bust with him when he came to the US, and it is still in the possession of his family. *(photo by James D. Perez)*

In spite of being one of Ambrosio's top stars and directors, the outbreak of World War I made Perez decide to leave Europe. His Robinet films were popular world-wide, with his character known as Tweedledum in the U.K. and America. Around one hundred and fifty-seven Robinet misadventures had been produced from 1910 to 1915 when Perez embarked for the United States. While records exist of an earlier 1910 Perez visit to Mexico and Arizona, it's not known if he had specific offers here in 1915, or if he just took a chance and came. Ellis Island records list him as arriving on May 26, 1915, and the first American credit that's been found for him is starring and co-directing with Allan Curtis the October 30, 1915 Joker one-reeler *A Day at Midland Beach*. Listed in the trade journal descriptions as Tweedledum, his connection with Joker and their distributor Universal appears to have very brief, for in January of 1916 it was announced:

> **BUNGLES IN VIM COMEDY**. Commencing Thursday, Feburary 27, Vim comedies will supersede MinA Comedies on the General Program. Bungles, the leading and most popular comedian in Europe, was forced on account of the war to cancel his contracts in Europe, and judging from his work in Vim comedies (the first of which will be *Bungles Rainy Day*, released on the General program February 10), he promises to soon become as famous and as great a success in this country as he has been abroad – second to none. He plays the leading parts in all his comedies, directs them, and writes his own scenarios. He has made a long contract to appear in Vim comedies. (*Moving Picture World*, January 15, 1916).

Bungles, it turns out, "is Fernandea Perez, a world famous comedian, recently from Italy, formerly known as 'Tweedledum,' the world famous fun-maker," but the long contract with Vim turned out to be only four shorts – *Bungles' Rainy Day*, *Bungles Enforces the Law*, *Bungles' Elopement*, and *Bungles Lands a Job* (all early 1916). Formed by Louis

Burstein, who later started King Bee, Vim turned out one-reelers with Bobby Burns and Walter Stull as Pokes and Jabbs, but their real claim to fame was the presence of a young Oliver Hardy, who worked with Burns and Stull but was soon teamed with Billy Ruge for a series of Plump and Runt Comedies. Other Vim players included Harry Myers, Rosemary Theby, Raymond McKee, Kate Price, Billy Bletcher, Ethel Burton, and Helen Gilmore. Hardy appeared in the four Bungles comedies, as did Elsie McLeod as Perez's leading lady.

Sadly, none of the Bungles are known to exist, but contemporary reviews were very favorable. Surviving photos show Perez looking very different than he did as Robinet, sporting a big moustache and eyebrows. Perez was reported to have made a close study of American comedies, at the time of his employment at Vim, when Mack Sennett's Keystone Comedies were the gold standard to which other comedies were compared. It's possible that Bungles' sprouting of facial hair was prompted by the fact that almost all of Sennett's popular clowns wore huge moustaches, goatees, etc. After the four shorts, Perez moved on and no info has surfaced on the break. Although fluent in Spanish, Italian, and French, Perez spoke no English on arrival in America and initially had to direct through an interpreter, so perhaps language complications soured the relationship with the studio.

Vim was in Jacksonville, Florida, which at the time was a beehive of comedy film production. Besides Vim there was, or would soon be, Lubin, Jaxon, Gaumont, Kalem, Klever Komedies, King Bee, Josh Binney Comedies, Sunbeam Comedies, and Cuckoo Comedies all in the vicinity. By June of 1916 Perez resurfaced at another Jacksonville concern, the Eagle Film Company. Eagle had been formed in Chicago under the supervision of William J. Dunn and moved to Florida in December of 1915. They were making *The Adventures of Duffy* and *Grogan's Alley* comedy shorts when Perez was hired to be their star attraction.

The films were released through the Unity Sales Corporation on a states' rights basis, which meant that instead of being released on one date nationwide the film's distribution rights were broken up into different territories and sold individually. For instance the Merit Film Corp. might start showing a short on Feb. 15 in Northern New Jersey while the Liberty Film Renting Co. might buy the rights for the same short a little later and not start showing it in the Pittsburgh area until June 15. Usually a states' rights company would sell a series of ten or twelve shorts for the year and make half right away. Then they'd complete the rest after a sufficient number of territories had been sold. All of Perez's future starring work would be in states' rights series, which often makes it difficult to pinpoint when an individual comedy was actually first released or for how long it played, as each of the films would circulate for a while in different parts of the country.

For his Eagle films, Perez got rid of the Bungles facial hair, and used the name under which he had been previously known in the U.S. – Tweedledum. Continuing with his basic Robinet character, he's a bungler who's always in trouble, but is wily and clever enough to come up with incredible schemes to get himself off the hook. *A Busy Night* (1916) is a tour-de-force which starts out with Tweedy getting inebriated while out on the town. Returning home to sleep it off, he has a nightmare which is a love triangle melodrama where he plays all the different roles – something like sixteen characters – so he not only makes love to himself, but ends up chasing himself from room to room as lover and irate husband. The special effects are wonderfully realized and are seamless, without a visual hitch or change in the lighting when the camera had to be stopped and then re-started. It's a huge leap from some of the primitive effects he had been doing in his European films like *Robinet Boxeur* (1913) and looks good even by today's standards.

A recent rediscovery is *A Bathtub Elopement* (1916) which turned up just months ago in a collection acquired by Library of Congress. Nilde Baracchi had joined Perez in America, billed as Tweedledee, and co-stars in this film as Jennie who lives on a farm with her over-bearing parents. Her folks insist that she marry goofy farmhand Andy, but she prefers goofy farmhand Tweedy. Basically a Florida-set version of Romeo and Juliet, Tweedy and Tweedledee manage to elude her parents by the use of funny and outrageous gags, and make their final escape by setting sail in a handy bathtub. Baracchi was re-named Babette Perez for this series, and described as Mrs. Perez in trade and newspaper items, but as they were both listed as single on official documents like ship's logs, etc., it appears that they were never married. The annoying parents are played by Louise Carver and Tom Murray, husband and wife vaudevillians who would eventually move to California and become silent comedy regulars. Other members of the Eagle stock company included J. Melvin Andrews (who was also a cameraman), Rex Adams, and Billy Slade.

Besides *A Busy Night* and *A Bathtub Elopement*, at least two other shorts survive from the total eleven Eagles made, and are the original Perez titles that I saw at MoMA. *Lend Me Your Wife* (1916) has Tweedy broke and facing the prospect of marrying his ugly landlady Louise Carver (a fate worse than death) to keep from being evicted. Getting a telegram that says his rich uncle Tom Murray is going to visit and bring him a large chunk of money if he is married, Tweedy makes a deal with a buddy to borrow his wife, in addition to the pal coming along to play their servant. Uncle comes and treats the servant badly, who in turn gets mad seeing Tweedy get too friendly with his wife. Finally uncle catches the wife and servant together in a compromising situation and the jig is up, but in the end Tweedy bites the bullet and marries the landlady and gets uncle's blessing.

Some Hero (1916) is a hilarious spoof of serial cliffhangers that has Tweedledee kidnapped and tortured by a gang of thugs with Tweedy in hot pursuit to save her. Full of wonderful cartoon gags, at one point when Tweedledee is tied up in a basement that's filling up with water, Tweedy drinks it all in order to save her and then sprays it out of his mouth like a fire hose to douse the crooks senseless. The last of the Eagle comedies was *The Near-Sighted Auto Pedist* (1916), an update of his previous *The Short-Sighted Cyclist*, and although the series was well-received and popular with much coverage and good reviews in exhibitor magazines, Eagle went into bankruptcy at the very end of 1916.

It appears that for at least a while, Perez remained in Jacksonville making films, but solid information on this period is very scant. According to the trade magazines, Perez joined comedian Harry Myers in forming Encore Pictures in January of 1917 and appeared at the Jacksonville Screen Club Ball on February 13, 1917, along with Myers, Oliver Hardy, and Victor Moore. One film that may have been made in this interim is a Tweedledum comedy titled *Two of a Kind*, which is listed as a Jockey Comedy and distributed by Unicorn. Lasting in the business for about a year, Unicorn specialized in, according to an item in the trades, "one and two reel subjects, dramas, comedies, and westerns, intended primarily to be used by exhibitors to balance feature programs," and is mostly remembered for having released a few of Chaplin imitator Billy West's first comedies. The supporting cast of *Two of a Kind* is made up of Babette Perez, Tom Murray, and Rex Adams, so it appears that either Perez was able to reassemble some of his Eagle crew or that the short was purchased when Eagle went bankrupt. Hopefully, more items and titles will surface to give a fuller story.

In 1918 and 1919, Perez starred in a two-year series of Jester Comedies produced by William Steiner and shot in Cliffside, New Jersey at studios formerly used by Kalem, with a brief foray to San Antonio, Texas. Steiner was a longtime independent producer and was known as "Big Bill" in the industry. He had never been involved with comedies before and in 1918 told the *Moving Picture World*:

Here I have been manufacturing film of every description but comedies for the past twenty-five years. Up to a few months ago if you mentioned the word 'comedy' I felt as if I wanted to fight, but now it is different. The work I find very interesting and to my liking. With Twede-Dan as my comedian I have a 'find.' Not only is he an unusual comedian with a style that is original and all his own, but he possesses a dramatic touch that is not often found in a man doing his class of work.

Steiner released the shorts on a states' right basis and used what he dubbed the "show you" policy. Most independent producers would have one or two advance screenings for buyers and critics, but Steiner had repeated screenings of completed comedies for exhibitors to view. Perez and Steiner also altered his screen character's name:

TWEDE-DAN IS TWEEDLEDUM. William "Big Bill" Steiner says the jig is up – he has been caught with the goods – and confesses that Twede-Dan, appearing in Jester Comedies, is none other than Tweedledum of European fame, prominent in the comedy field several years ago appearing in pictures released under Pathé, Eclipse, Éclair and Ambrosio brands.

Twede-Dan, as he is now known to the American movie-goer, has now been in this country for nearly two years, and has spent the greater part of that time studying the American methods of making pictures and developing a new line of comedy, as shown in the first three Jester releases, "The Recruit," "His Golden Romance," and "All Fur Her." Today we see Tweedledum, alias Twede-Dan, doing things the American way. It was hard at first, but now he is presented as a real American type of actor with a distinct line of comedy (*Moving Picture World*, April 13, 1918).

Nilde Baracchi returned as his leading lady, through rechristened Nilde Babette for this series, and for some reason it was decided to tell the press that she had just arrived in America despite the fact that she had appeared in the Eagle comedies. The April 16, 1918 *Moving Picture World* reported:

Nilde Babette, appearing as a leading comedienne opposite Twede-Dan in Jester comedies, while a newcomer in America is not new in the film art, as she has appeared in many pictures made in France and Italy, and also acted on the stage in Paris. Miss Babette has only been in this country for a few months, but is fast becoming Americanized, and what little she has seen of America thus far she proclaims as most charming. She has seen a great deal of the war in Europe, and has several brothers in the French army and a number of sisters with the French Red Cross.

The series began in February and in March, Thomas C. Regan, who had been an assistant director with Pathé, Mittenthal, Pokes and Jabbs, and the World Film Company, was engaged as assistant director and part-time actor. In June, William A. Seiter came in to direct the series. Seiter, well-remembered today for his silent comedies with Reginald Denny and Laura La Plante, and many talking films like *Sons of the Desert* (1934), came to Jester from directing Chaplin imitator Ray Hughes for Pyramid Comedies and would leave before the Jesters were over to direct Mr. and Mrs. Carter De Haven for producer William "Smiling Billy" Parsons at Capitol Comedies. Seiter and Perez would work together again at Universal in 1927. Reviews for the comedies were very good and Steiner appears to have had great success in selling the series, so much so that in October he announced that he was adding Jimmy Aubrey and Pearl Sheppard in a new group of comedies. A lobby card has turned up with Aubrey and Sheppard in a Jester entitled *The Fatal Flower*, but it seems that these additions were short-lived and by 1919 it was only Twede-Dan again.

Out of the twenty-five Jester Comedies produced, only five are known to exist today. The only two from the first season are the second reel of *Camouflage* (1918) at the Library of Congress, in which Tweedy is a detective who thinks Nilde is a German spy and trails her all over town to a meeting with the Kaiser himself, which turns out to only be a movie being shot. Although only the second half of the film, it's a great example of Perez's work, with some amazing gags, surreal situations, and the loose, off-the-cuff feel of his European days. The Museum of Modern Art has the other first season survivor, a chunk of the first reel of *Oh, What a Day!* (1918), which chronicles Tweedy and Nilde's problems when their car breaks down on their way to a seaside resort. When they find that they're out of gas, Tweedy uses booze for fuel but then has to deal with a drunken car.

In the fall of 1918, producer Steiner rented the facilities of Sunset Pictures in San Antonio, Texas. While the company was shooting westerns they also made a few Jester shorts such as *A Mexican Mix-Up, The Wisest Fool,* and *The Tenderfoot* (all 1919). In the surviving second reel of *The Tenderfoot,* Tweedy has gone out west and fallen in love with pretty cowgirl Nilde, but Wildcat Winnie, the unattractive saloon owner, wants him for herself. She ties him up in a shed next to a lit keg of dynamite and makes him chose between her and death. Tweedy picks death, but luckily Nilde comes to the rescue.

This seems to be one of Nilde Baracchi's last appearances. With her leaving the company and returning to Europe, there were more changes in the personnel of the shorts, including a new leading lady. The spot was filled by the twenty-two year-old Ithaca girl Esther Elmendorf, who was luckily renamed Dorothy Earle. She not only became Perez's co-star for the remainder of his comedy shorts, but married him in real life.

An important addition to the supporting stock company was the gigantic, 342-pound Belgian Jean Pierre Pierard. The bald-domed Pierard was not only a former circus performer and wrestler (where he was billed as La Collosse or Pierre Collosse), but also, like Perez, was a veteran of early European films for Pathé and Éclipse. It's unknown if he and Perez had known each other in Europe, but La Collosse would remain as Perez's Mack Swain through his Reelcraft shorts. As his large size and shiny head made him a perfect comedy heavy, he also worked for other east coast-based companies such as Vitagraph, Gaumont, Pyramid, and even in features on the order of

Manhandled (1924) with Gloria Swanson. His last known appearance is in the Charley Bowers short *Many a Slip* (1926).

By the second season of the Jesters producer Steiner is calling his production company Territorial Sales Corporation and, while still doing the comedies, is expanding into features and two-reel westerns. There's much less publicity and reviews for the Twede-Dans as if Steiner was letting the series run on its own steam while he actively promoted new projects. The two other existing Jester comedies are some of the best examples of his American work. *You're Next* (1919) has Perez thrown out of his flat and taking up residence with all his furniture in the middle of a street. Since he's tying up traffic cops come and tell him to move, but take pity on him and let him set up housekeeping in the jailhouse. After throwing a wild party there, he's back on the street where he meets Dorothy, herself a victim of lack of rent money. When she gets hired to act in a movie, Tweedy comes along as general studio gofer and, of course, causes all sorts of problems during shooting. The second reel of this gem is set in the Jester Studio and gives a wonderful behind the scenes tour.

Recently restored by George Eastman House is *Can You Beat It?* (1919). Tweedy is engaged to fat rich girl Angelica, and after trying to put up with her jumbo-sized and annoying family for the sake of the money, he ends up with Angelica's cute maid Ninette. The Twede-Dan series ended at the end of 1919, although the finished shorts continued to be distributed into the early 1920s.

Instead of going straight to a new series of shorts, Perez embarked on something new – directing features. Although he would seem a natural to direct slapstick features, in 1920 there really weren't any. Mabel Normand and Roscoe Arbuckle were the only comics who had jumped from shorts to features but these were polite, situational comedies with a few sight gags used as occasional seasoning. Instead, Perez directed two society dramas that William Steiner was involved in producing for the independent market. *The Way of Women* (1920) and *Luxury* (1921) both starred Rubye de Remer, a former Ziegfeld beauty who had recently entered films. One reel of *The Way of Women* survives at Library of Congress and is a very enjoyable melodrama of grand passions, with acting gestures to match. It was during this period that he settled on the name Marcel Perez. He may have thought it sounded a little fancier for features and he kept it for the rest of his career. Another event that happened at this time was the birth of a son, Marcel Jr., to he and Dorothy.

As a performer he hadn't made any new films for almost a year and a half, but on April 9, 1921, the *Moving Picture World* announced:

TWEEDY DAN WITH REELCRAFT. Tweedy Dan, known on both sides of the Atlantic as a comedian, is to be the star of two-reel comedies to be distributed by Reelcraft Pictures Corporation. The organization for the series has been completed and the first picture is now being made at the Mittenthal Studio in Yonkers. Tweedy Dan was one of the first actors to appear before the camera. He was with Pathé for five years then with Éclair, and later with Ambrosio in Italy, where he was featured comedian in a series of one-reel comedies distributed throughout the world, and which proved to be very popular. He became director-general of that company and later came to the United States and was featured in a series of Jester Comedies for William Steiner. His efforts have been recently confined to directing, having produced a series of features under the name of Marcel Perez.

Reelcraft was a distribution company that specialized in comedy shorts. It was formed in 1920 when the Bulls Eye Film Co., the Emerald Motion Picture Co., and the Bee Hive Film Exchange merged. The president was R.C. Cropper and the company released the films of popular comics such as Alice Howell, Billy West, Gale Henry, and Milburn Moranti. They also handled people completely forgotten today, like William and Gordon Dooley, Frederic J. Ireland, and Billy B. Van, in addition to picking up stray shorts such as Stan Laurel's *The Lucky Dog* (1921) for distribution.

Twede-Dan was soon shortened to Tweedy and the series was named Mirth Comedies. Perez joined Reelcraft during its later days. The bigger names were gone and most of the product was being made by Schiller Productions. Morris and Julius Schiller produced Perez's Mirth Comedies, plus Aladdin Comedies starring Bud Duncan and Sun-Lite Comedies with Billy Quirk (and a young Jobyna Ralston). Although the Sun-Lites were mostly shot in Florida, the Schiller's home base was in Yonkers, NY, and the Mirths and Aladdins were shot there at the old Mittenthal Studio.

Rejoined by Dorothy and Pierre Collosse as support, four of the Mirth Comedies are known to exist today. The Library of Congress has *Sweet Daddy* (1921), which is one of his very best surviving films. Tweedy is a henpecked husband whose militant suffragette wife keeps him chained by the neck to the kitchen wall doing dishes. When he tries to stand up for himself, she shoves him out the window and there are hilarious shots of him hanging by his neck three stories up in the air. The wife finally hauls him back in and sends him on an errand to the grocery. On the way, he passes billboards for a musical show and in a charming scene, he imagines the girl in the photo comes to life, so he flirts with her and gives her a kiss. Continuing on his way, he comes across the real girl on the poster being accosted by a couple of thugs and he comes to her rescue. Smitten, he goes to see her in the show and afterward, they go to a restaurant together.

Tweedy is having a great time eating spaghetti with his sweetie when his wife comes in with her suffragette friends and sit at an adjoining table. Tweedy's in a panic but gets a plan. He sends Dorothy out and when she comes back she's dressed as a nurse and begins wrapping Tweedy in bandages. His alibi is that he's been in an accident. At first, it works as his wife frantically sends for a doctor, but soon she catches on and everything hits the fan, which results in a marvelous chase. Tweedy, whose lower half is wrapped like a mummy, literally hops through the whole chase, in and out of rooms, up and down stairs, etc. Although it's hard to describe and really needs to be seen, it's quite a feat of athletics and is very clever, and riotously funny. Finally Tweedy gets cornered by his wife and the doctor, who grab ends of the bandages which spins him around like a top. The film's big set piece is Dorothy's musical show which was shot at Yonkers' Proctor Theatre (today a bank) during a special "Schiller Night," where performances were given by Tweedy, Billy Quirk, and Bud Duncan, in addition to the audience participating in the shooting of *Sweet Daddy*.

The first reel of *Weekend* (1921) chronicles Tweedy's misadventures when he and Dorothy get invited to a weekend in the country. Besides missing the excursion boat, when Tweedy gets pulled into the water while fishing and crashes over rocks and a waterfall, all he has to show for a catch is an old boot. *Pinched* and *Wild* (both 1921) are the two other surviving Reelcrafts, and while *Pinched* has yet to be viewed, *Wild* is a spoof of rough and ready westerns, where our hero Tweedy catches bullets in his teeth and drop-kicks half ton boulders to bean the villains. The Reelcraft series shows that Perez continued to refine his comic persona. In *Sweet Daddy*, there's a touch of pathos and wistfulness in his mistreatment by his wife and a lot of charm in the scene where he imagines that the girl on the poster has come to life. At least sixteen Mirth two-reelers were made. In addition Perez directed a number of Aladdin Comedies, one-reelers such as *Fireworks*, *Blowing Bubbles*, and *Shot* (all 1921), that featured Billy Moran and Dorothy Earle.

Reelcraft ceased production in late fall of 1921. Looking through exhibitor magazines of the time, there's progressively less and less items on the Reelcraft product, then after November, nothing. Finally, an item in the June 17, 1922 *Moving Picture World* reports:

BANKRUPTCY INVOLVES REELCRAFT. New York – An involuntary petition was filed here on Wednesday June 7, against Reelcraft Pictures Corporation, a producing and distribution company with offices at 220 West 42nd Street, on the complaint of three creditors. Nothing in the petition filed disclosed the identity of those connected with the corporation in an official or other capacity, but the complaint alleges the liabilities are $150,000 and the assets $50,000. Judge John C. Knox appointed Max Cedarbaum receiver for the concern with a bond of $2,500.

This was followed on October 28, 1922, with:

EXPORT-IMPORT BUYS REELCRAFT. Export & Import Film Company, Inc., this week announced that it had purchased from the receivers of the Reelcraft Pictures Corporation all rights, title, and interest in negatives in the possession of the latter firm. These negatives embrace 160 in number, including one and two-reel subjects with Billy West, Texas Guinan, Billy Franey, Matty Roubert, George Clarke, and Milburn Moranti comedies.

With Reelcraft out of commission, Perez turns up in the spring of 1922 working for producer F.M. Sanford to direct a series of eight western features starring Pete Morrison and a new group of twelve Tweedy comedies. Unfortunately, only four of the Morrison features and six Tweedy shorts, that included *Fire-Fire*, *Take a Tip*, and *Friday the 13th* (all 1922), were completed.

At the end of 1922, a cancerous tumor was found in his leg, resulting in it being amputated at the knee. Director Robert Florey wrote in his 1948 memoir *Hollywood d'hier et ajjourd'hui* that Perez told him that the amputation occurred due to an accident that happened while making one of his Sanford comedies. While shooting a scene, he fell on an upturned rake. The teeth of the rake sank into his leg and penetrating the bone leading to amputation. But according to Perez's death certificate the leg operation was due to cancer, a cancer that would return a few years later.

Perez seems to have been out of commission starting in early 1923. Some of the films he had recently made for Sanford continued to be in distribution while he was recovering. His return to the film industry came in 1924 working behind the scenes, directing and writing Jimmy Aubrey comedies for producer Joe Rock and his Standard Cinema Corporation. Rock was a well-known comic who, after producing his own starring shorts for a few years, more or less retired as a performer to produce series with other comics like Aubrey and Stan Laurel. Unfortunately, specific credits weren't given on the Aubrey series so it's not known exactly which titles Perez worked on, but the trade magazines document his contributions to the series.

By 1925, Rock was concentrating on two series – Standard Comedies, also known as Fat Men Comedies, starring Frank "Fatty" Alexander, Hilliard "Fatt" Karr, and William "Kewpie" Ross, and Blue Ribbon Comedies with Alice Ardell, who was billed as "Joe Rock's latest find" and "a young Parisian girl who it is prophesied will be one of the screen sensations of the year." Perez began directing the Ardell series with its third comedy *Hold Tight* (1925). A gimmick for the series was having a different male comedian play opposite Ardell in each short. So Chester Conklin, Lee Moran, Slim Summerville, Neely Edwards, and Joe Rock himself took turns appearing as well as supplying most of the laughs. Ms. Ardell was pretty, athletic, and had a pleasing personality – but wasn't funny. The shorts are funny due to the talents of people like Perez behind the camera and of Ardell's leading men and supporting comics on the screen.

Historian Sam Gill opines that Perez may have been brought in to direct the bulk of these comedies because Ardell only spoke French and Perez was fluent in it. Publicity items for the films usually noted that "Tweedy, who is handling the megaphone, was once a comedian" or "this production was directed by Marcel Perez, himself a well-known comedian and better known to film fans as 'Tweedy.'" Surviving entries such as *Hold Tight*, and *A Peaceful Riot* (both 1925) show a strong directorial hand. The shorts clip along at a nice pace and there are many large physical comedy set pieces which are directed with snap and precision.

It's definite that Perez directed six of the Ardells and one of the Fat Men comedies, but it's probable that he worked on more. Besides the Rock-produced shorts, he resumed directing independent features, mostly low-budget westerns, such as *Pioneers of the West* (1925) with Dorothy as the female lead (plus a cameo by Marcel, Jr.) and *Lash of the Law* (1926), where he took a final acting role as the heroine's crippled brother. Perez worked on the Rock comedies until early 1926 and then entered the last phase of his career:

UNIVERSAL PLANS FIFTY-TWO COMEDIES. A comedy schedule which includes fifty-two one-reel pictures for the next twelve months has been adopted by Universal.

Arthur Lake will make thirteen "Sweet Sixteen" comedies under the direction of George Summerville. An additional thirteen two-reelers will be done by Charles Puffy under the direction of Dick Smith. Neely Edwards will do thirteen with no director chosen for him as yet. "Slim" Summerville and "Fanny" the mule are also on the list for a series of thirteen novelty comedies.

Four comedy constructors have been engaged by Scott Darling, head of the comedy units, to write and assist in the production of the stories. They are Eugene De Rue, Marcel Perez, Frederick Spencer, and Charles Diltz. (*Motion Picture News*, May 22, 1926).

As a "comedy constructor", Perez not only worked on the Universal shorts but also wrote for old collaborator William Seiter's features *Out All Night* (with a good role for Dorothy) and *The Small Bachelor* (both 1927). His last directorial effort was the Charles Puffy two-reeler *His In Laws*, which was released on March 12, 1928, but had been made earlier and copyrighted on October 19, 1927. The cancer that caused the amputation of his leg returned in 1927 as a tumor in his left lung. For a description of his last days, we go back to Robert Florey's memoir. Florey said that he had gone to a hospital to visit actress Renée Adorée. While at the hospital, he found out that Perez was there and had been for six weeks. He was near death and the doctors had kept the seriousness of his condition from him. Perez and Florey talked at length about Charles Prince, Max Linder, André Deed, and other friends from Pathé. Florey said that Perez died ten days later, alone and ignored.

He died on February 8, 1929 at the Windsor Hospital in Glendale, and wasn't entirely alone and ignored, as he had Dorothy and nine year-old Marcel, Jr. By 1930, the two were living in Manhattan, where Dorothy was working as a hotel hostess and living with her mother and aunt. In 1936 she remarried, and passed away in 1958 in Los Angeles. Marcel, Jr. died in 1996 at age seventy-five. But alone and ignored is a good description of how Perez has been treated by posterity, thanks mainly to his confusion of names and the amount of missing films. Happily, after decades of neglect, the last few years have seen a resurgence of interest with information on his life and career finally coming to the fore. Many films have been found, and a number of his European shorts have even become readily available online. Now we have *The Marcel Perez* Collection, a DVD of some of his best surviving comedies, sort of a Perez sampler, giving silent comedy fans the opportunity to enjoy his work and become acquainted with his unique talents.

Vim Company
photo from the
*Motion Picture
News* with
Perez second
from left in the
second row as
Fernandez
Perez

VIM COMEDY COMPANY. Bottom row, left to right: BERT TRACY, ROY GAHRIS, HARRY NAUGHTON. Second row: WILL LOUIS, FERNANDEZ PEREZ (BUNGLES), EDWARD McWADE, LOUIS BURSTEIN, BABE HARDY, BILLY RUGE, BOBBY BURNS, WALTER STULL.

Jacksonville, Florida's Eagle Film Studio in 1916. It later became the Norman Studios and is still standing today. *Courtesy of James Snaden and family*

Perez slugs Billy Slade as Louise Carver (left), Rex Adams (below), and Nilde Baracchi stand by in *Torpedoed by Cupid* (1916). *Courtesy of James Snaden and family*

Promotional still for *A Busy Night* (1916), showing Perez with all the characters he plays in the film. *Courtesy of James Snaden and family.*

Candid shot from the Jester Studio of assistant director/actor Thomas C. Regan (left), producer William "Big Bill" Steiner (middle), and character comedienne Jane Wills. *Courtesy of Robert S. Birchard*

Behind the scenes at the Jester Studio in Cliffside, New Jersey with Jane Wills (left), Thomas C. Regan (left in checkered cap), Perez and Nilde Baracchi with backs to camera, and producer William Steiner (right in derby). *Courtesy of Robert S. Birchard*

Action scene from *This is the Life* (1918) with Thomas C. Regan doing his best to get away from Jane Wills as Nilde Baracchi and Perez look on. *Courtesy of Robert S. Birchard*

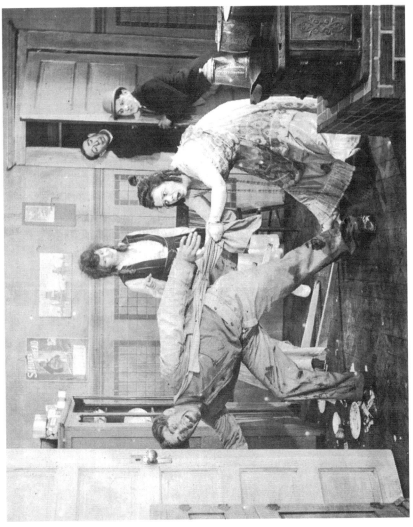

A beautiful shot of Nilde Baracchi (a.k.a. Babette Perez, Nilde Babette, etc., etc.) in a lobby card for 1918's *The Fly Ball. Courtesy of Sam Gill*

An unusual shot of Perez wearing glasses á la Harold Lloyd from *The Fly Ball* (1918). *Courtesy of Sam Gill.*

Twede-Dan
surrounded by
business pressures in
The Tenderfoot (1919).
*Courtesy of Robert S.
Birchard.*

Title lobby card for *A Mexican Mix-Up* (1919), one of the Jesters shot in San Antonio, Texas. *Courtesy of Sam Gill.*

Twede-Dan shocks
Nilde Baracchi (rear
center) with his
attentions to Jane
Wills (left) in 1919's
A Mexican Mix-Up.
Courtesy of Sam Gill

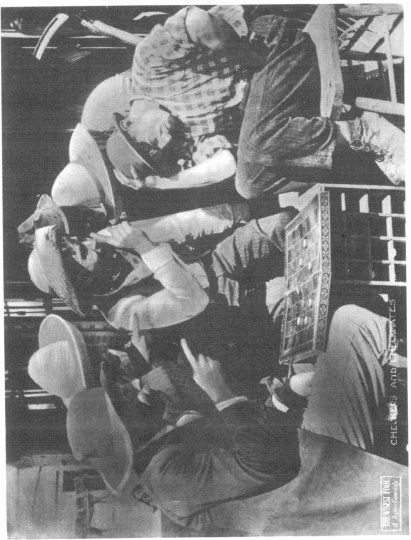

Perez failing at checkers in *The Wisest Fool* (1919). *Courtesy of Sam Gill.*

Looks like a happy ending for Twede-Dan in 1919's *The Wisest Fool. Courtesy of Sam Gill.*

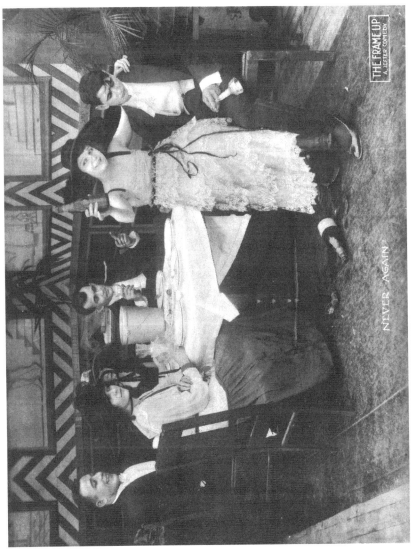

Looks like too much wine, women, and song for Twede-Dan in 1919's *The Frame-Up*. *Courtesy of Sam Gill.*

Perez surrounded by Dorothy Earle and a bevy of beauties in *Chicken in Turkey* (1919). *Courtesy of Sam Gill.*

Twede-Dan at left in drag seems to be trying to protect Dorothy from Pierre Collosse (second from left) in *Chicken in Turkey* (1919). *Courtesy of Sam Gill.*

Perez and Nilde Baracchi (left) have their version of dinner in an unidentified Jester comedy. *Courtesy of Cole Johnson.*

Perez looking snappy for his first Reelcraft release in 1921. *Courtesy of Sam Gill.*

Tweedy set to conk the bad guy and rescue Dorothy Earle in *Here He Is* (1921). *Courtesy of Sam Gill.*

Dorothy Earle and Perez have picked up an unwanted rider in *Vacation* (1921). *Courtesy of Cole Johnson.*

Title lobby card for
1921's *Moving*.
Courtesy of Sam Gill.

Tweedy should have used a better transfer company in *Moving* (1921). Long-time Mack Sennett stuntman and comic Billy Gilbert is the second mover on the left. *Courtesy of Sam Gill.*

Tweedy takes aim at Pierre Collosse as Dorothy Earle looks on in *Moving* (1921). *Courtesy of Sam Gill.*

Lobby card for 1921's *Week End*, the first reel of which exists at the EYE Filmmuseum in the Netherlands. *Courtesy of Sam Gill.*

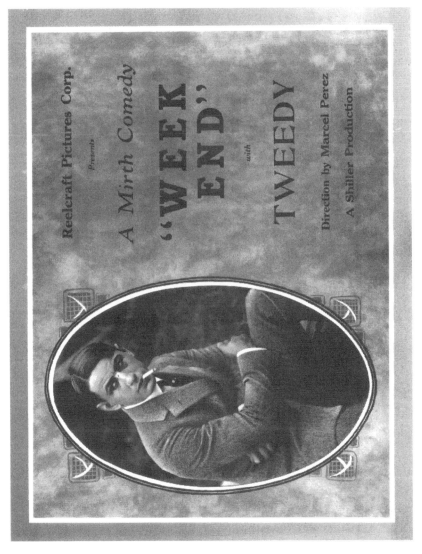

Perez and Dorothy have a quiet moment at home in *Week End* (1921). *Courtesy of Sam Gill.*

The beggar is only one of Tweedy's obstacles in trying to take a pleasure trip in *Week End* (1921). *Courtesy of Sam Gill.*

Tweedy plays a plumber's helper in his Reelcraft comedy *Pinched* (1921) with support from Pierre Collasse (left), Dorothy Earle, and Billy Moran (right). *Author's collection.*

Lobby card for Perez's last starring comedy *Friday the 13th* (1923). *Author's collection.*

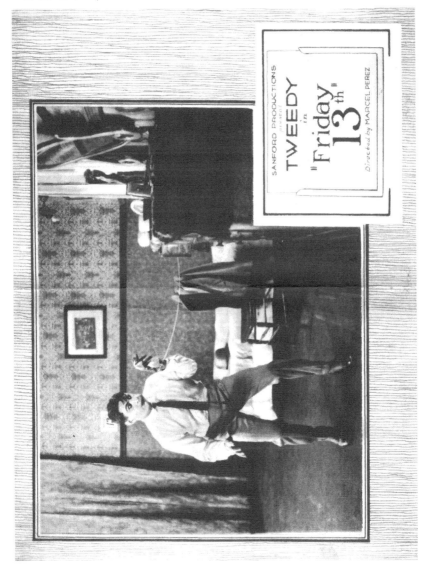

Perez (right of camera) and crew shooting *Mummy Love* (1926) in the courtyard of Grauman's Egyptian Theatre. Actors in foreground are from left to right Yorke Sherwood, Neely Edwards, Alice Ardell, and Frederick Peters. *Marc Wanamaker/Bison Archives*

Closer view of production still: Perez directing *Mummy Love* (1926) with crutches at his side. *Marc Wanamaker/ Bison Archives.*

Behind the scenes shot during the making of the western feature *Pioneers of the West* (1925). Perez is all the way to the left sitting in chair. Others include Bud Osborne (third from left), Olin Francis (tall Indian in back), Dick Carter (third from right in black hat), Dorothy Earle (second from right), Elmer Dyer (right), and Gene Crosby (sitting on ground right). *Courtesy of Robert S. Birchard.*

Closer view of production still: Perez on the set of *Pioneers of the West* (1925) with back to camera to hide his missing leg. Little boy under the tripod is four year-old Marcel Perez Jr. *Courtesy of Robert S. Birchard.*

FILMOGRAPHY

Filmography Key:
PD=Producer, Dist=Distributor, C=Cast, A=Author,
D=Director, PH=Photographer, WT=Working Title

CB=Cineteca di Bologna, Italy
CF=Cineteca del Friuli, Italy
CI=Cineteca Italiana, Milan
CN=Cineteca Nazionale, Roma
CNC=CNC French Film Archives, Bois d'Arcy
CQ=La Cinematheque Quebecoise, Canada
DF=Det Danske Filmmuseum, Denmark
EYE=Eye Film Institute Netherlands, Amsterdam
FCA=Fundacion Cinematea Argentina, Buenos Aires
GEH=George Eastman House, Rochester, New York
LOB=Lobster Films, Paris
LOC=Library of Congress, Washington, DC
MC=Museo de Cinema, Turin
MoMA=Museum of Modern Art, New York
NFA/BFI=National Film Archive, London
NFC=National Film Center, Tokyo

An asterisk denotes that a film is known to exist.

This a game attempt at charting Perez's prolific output. Much more information needs to be found, especially on his early European films and the period of 1917 in America.

PART ONE: EARLY EUROPEAN FILMS

Perez began his film career around 1900 at Pathe, and through 1910 also worked for Eclipse, Eclair, and Gaumont. Sadly, at the moment, all of these early titles are unknown except for the following three:

*Les Devaliseurs Noctures** (1904) PD: Pathé. D: Gaston Velle. (Also known as Burglars at Work. Released in the United States in 1908 as *Nocturnal Thieves*) (CNC)
*The Short-Sight Cyclist** (1907) PD: Eclipse. (MoMA, NFA/BFI)
*La Police l'an 2000** (1910) (*Police in the Year 2000*) PD: Gaumont. C: Perez, Eugene Breon, Clement Mege. (EYE)

AS ROBINET FOR AMBROSIO CO. OF TURIN

1910
Il Capoanno di Robinet
*Il Duello di Robinet** *(Tweedledum's Duel)* (CN)
Frigot Impiegato Municipale
Gigetta al Reggimento (*Molly at the Regiment*) C: Gigetta Morano.
Gigetta si Vendica di Robinet C: Gigetta Morano.
Ossessione de Robinet per il Ballo
*La Prima Bicicletta di Robinet** (*Tweedledum's First Bicycle*) (EYE)
Il Prurito di Robinet (*Fricot's Itching Powder*)
Robinet Ama la Figlia del Generale
Robinet Appassionato pei Dirigibile (*Tweedledum's Aeronautical Adventure*)
Robinet Costretto a Fare il Ladro (*Tweedledum's Forged Banknote*)

Robinet ha il Sonno Duro* *(Tweedledum's Sleeping Sickness)* (CN, LOC)

Robinet ha la Mania del Savadanio

Robinet ha Perso il Treno *(Tweedledum Has Missed His Train)*

Robinet ha un Tic per il Ballo

Robinet Questerino *(Trials of Tweedledum as a Policeman)*

Robinet Studia una Parte Tragica *(Tweedledum Learns a Tragical Part)*

Robinet Vuol Fare il Jockey* *(Tweedledum wants to be a Jockey)* (EYE)

Storia di un Paio di Stivali

1911

L'Abito Bianco di Robinet* *(Tweedledum's White Suit)* (EYE)

L'Astuzia di Robinet *(Artful Tweedledum)*

L'Auto di Robinet* *(Tweedledum's Motor Car)* (EYE, MC)

Gli Auto-Scat di Robinet* *(Tweedledum's Auto-Skates)* (LOC)

Un Avventura di Robinet

La Cintura D'Oro

La Collana Rubata *(The Necklace Affair)*

La Furberie di Robinet* *(Tweedledum and one of his Tricks)* (EYE)

Gastone e Robinet Vogolino Prender Moglie *(Tweedledum and Frosty Want to Get Married)*

Il Pesce D'Aprile di Robinet *(Tweedledum's April Fool Joke)*

Reclame del Sarto

Robinet Ammiratore di Napoleone *(Exploits of a Napoleon Admirer)*

Robinet Arriva in Ritardo *(Tweedledum is Late)*

Robinet Aviatore* (CF, CI)

Robinet Detective

Robinet e il Monocolo della Verita C: Nilde Baracchi.

Robinet e L'Avventuriera *(Tweedledum and the Adventuress)*

Robinet e Troppo Timido *(Tweedledum is Shy)*

Robinet ed i Salvatori *(Tweedledum and his Rescuer)* C: Nilde Baracchi.

Robinet ha Rubato Centro Lire* (EYE)

Robinet in Bolletta* *(Tweedledum's Financial Distress)* (EYE)

Robinet in Societa (Tweedledum Goes into High Life)

Robinet Innamorato di una Chanteuse* (Tweedledum in Love with a Cabaret Singer) C: Gigetta Morano. (EYE, MC)

Robinet si Dedica Agli Sports Invernali* (Tweedledum Tries Winter Sports) (NFA/BFI)

Robinet Sposa un Americana (Tweedledum Marries an American Girl) C: Nilde Baracchi.

Robinet Tra due Fuochi* (NFA/BFI)

Robinet Vuol Diventare Eroe* (LOB)

Robinet Sua Moglie e il Cugino

Uno Scherzo di Robinet C: Nilde Baracchi.

La Scimmia di Robinet (Tweedledum's Monkey)

Il Sogno di Robinet* (Tweedledum's Dream) (DF)

Gil Stivali di Robinet (Tweedledum's Riding Boots) C: Nilde Baracchi.

1912

Un Complotto Contro Robinet

Una Dichiarazione Impossibile di Robinet* C; Nilde Baracchi. (EYE)

L'Evasione di Robinet (Tweedeldum's Evasion) C: Nilde Baracchi.

Nei Lacci del Destino

La Nuova Cameriera e Troppo Bella* (The New Maid is Too Much of a Flirt) C: Nilde Baracchi. (NFC)

Un Nuovo Furto di Robinet

L'Onomastico di Robinet C: Nilde Baracchi.

Le Rendite di Robinet C: Nilde Baracchi.

Robinet Alpino

Robinet Caricaturista C: Nilde Baracchi.

Robinet Commesso Viaggiatore

Robinet Contro un Rubinetto

Robinet Cycliste

Robinet Diventa un Ercole

Robinet fa il Giro D'Italia in Bicicletta

Robinet fa la Cura dei Bagni C: Nilde Baracchi.

Robinet fa un Allievo (The Actor's Test)

Robinet Falso Cow-Boy C: Nilde Baracchi.

Robinet Guida per Amore C: Nilde Baracchi.

Robinet in un Educandato* (NFA/BFI) C: Nilde Baracchi.

Robinet in Vacanza* (EYE, NFA/BFI) C: Nilde Baracchi.

Robinet Landro Inafferrabile C: Nilde Baracchi.

Robinet Maestro D'Equitazione (Tweedledum's Riding School)

Robinet Nichilista* (CI)

Robinet Operatore

Robinet Padre e Figlio* (Tweedledum's Father and his Worthy Son) (EYE)

Robinet Ricattatore* C: Nilde Baracchi. (EYE)

Robinet Ricco per Dieci Minuti* (EYE)

Robinet Scioperante

Robinet si Assicura Alla Vita (Tweedledum Insures His Life) C: Nilde Baracchi.

Robinet si Allena per il Giro D'Italia* (Tweedledum Practicing for a Bicycle Race) (CF, CI, NFA/BFI)

Robinet Sogna il Mare C: Nilde Baracchi.

Robinet Troppo Amato da sua Moglie* (Tweedledum is Too Much Loved By His Wife) C: Nilde Baracchi, Gigetta Morano. (EYE)

La Strenna di Robinet (Tweedledum's New Year's Gift)

Uno Zoppo chef a Strada

1913

Una Buona Giornata di Robinet

Cenerentola*

Come Robinet Sposo Robinette C: Nilde Baracchi.

Il Duello di Fricot* C: Nilde Baracchi. (CF, CN)

I Fratelli Robinet C: Nilde Baracchi.

Fricot Canatastorie C: Nilde Baracchi.

L'Idolo di Robinet

*Madamigella Robinet** C: Nilde Baracchi. (EYE, MC)

La Madre di Robinet C: Nilde Baracchi.

Robinet Arma la Fioraia C: Nilde Baracchi.

*Robinet Anarchico** *(Tweedledum as an Anarchist)*

Robinet Attaccato alla Sella

*Robinet Boxeur** (CF)

*Robinet Cocchiere** (CI)

Robinet Corteggiatore Tenace

Robinet e Butalin si Battono

Robinet e lo Steeple-Chase C: Nilde Baracchi.

Robinet Femminista C: Nilde Baracchi.

*Robinet Guardia Ciclista** (CF, MoMA) C: Nilde Baracchi.

Robinet Malato di Sonno

Robinet Poliziotto

*Robinet Reporter** (EYE)

Robinet Sbaglia Piano C: Nilde Baracchi.

Robinet si da alla Malavita

Robinet Sportsman

Robinet Sposa a Vapore C: Nilde Baracchi.

Robinet Studia Matematica C: Nilde Baracchi.

Robinet Tenore

Robinet Vuol Lavorare

Robinet Vuol Piantare un Chiodo

Robinet Vuol Sposare una Dote

Robinet, Robinette C: Nilde Baracchi.

Una Scommessa di Butalin e di Robinet C: Nilde Baracchi.

La Suocera di Robinet C: Nilde Baracchi.

ADVENTURE SERIAL FOR AMBROSIO

*Le Avventure Straordinarissime di Saturnino Farandola** (*The Extraordinary Adventures of Saturnino Farandola*) (1914) D: Marcel Fabre & Luigi Maggi. A: Guido Volante, from the novel by Ferdinand Robina. PH: Ottavio De Matteis. Art Dir: Enrico Lupi &

Decoroso Bonifanti. C: MF, Nilde Baracchi, Filippo Castamagna, Luciano Manara, Alfredo Bertone, Luigi Stinchi, Armando Pilotti, Dario Silvestri, Vittorio Tettoni, Oreste Grandi. (Originally released in four episodes: *The Isle of Monkeys*; *In Quest of the White Elephant*; *The Queen of Makalolos*; *Farandola Versus Phileas Fogg*). (Released in the U.S. as: *Zingo*; *Zingo and the White Elephant*; *Zingo in Africa*; *Zingo the Son of the Sea*; *Zingo's War in the Clouds*). (CI)

AS ROBINET FOR AMBROSIO

1914
*Amour Pedestre** (*Love Afoot*) (DF, CQ, FCA, MoMA)
L'Amore Diede la Forza a Robinet C: Nilde Baracchi.
Il Bastone di Robinet
Il Cavallo Fedele C: Nilde Baracchi.
Come Robinet Divento Comico C: Nilde Baracchi.
Delenda Carthago! (*The Destruction of Carthage*)
La Donne Economa C: Nilde Baracchi.
Duetto in Quattro C: Nilde Baracchi.
L'Energia di Fricot C: Nilde Baracchi.
Il Piccolo Fricot
Un Qui Pro Quo di Sheriff-Holfufus
Robinet alla Caccia della Volpe C: Nilde Baracchi.
Robinet ama Disinteressatamente C: Nilde Baracchi.
Robinet Cerca L'Ideale C: Nilde Baracchi.
*Robinet Chauffeur Miope** (EYE, MC)
*Robinet e Geloso** (*Robinet is Jealous*) C: Nilde Baracchi. (EYE)
*Robinet Fotografo** (CI)
Robinet ha del Crattere C: Nilde Baracchi.
Robinet ha il Tipo Americano C: Nilde Baracchi.
Robinet ha il Torcicollo
Robinet non Vuol Saperne C: Nilde Baracchi.
Robinet Perde e Guadagna C: Nilde Baracchi.

*Robinet Pescatore** (EYE)
La Trovata di Robinet C: Nilde Baracchi.
Un Viaggio Laborioso C: Nilde Baracchi.

1915
La Cambiale di Robinet
La Colpe del Morto C: Nilde Baracchi.
Concorrenza Spietata
Jack Forbes Contro Robinet C: Nilde Baracchi.
Il Paletot a Martingala di Robinet
Quando Robinet Ama C: Nilde Baracchi.
Robinet Angelo Custode C: Nilde Baracchi.
Robinet Detective Amateur C: Nilde Baracchi.
Robinet e il Conto del Pranzo
Robinet Muore per Amore C: Nilde Baracchi.
*Robinet Pescatore per Amore** C: Nilde Baracchi. (CB)
Robinet Torna a Robinette C: Nilde Baracchi.
Robinette Vuol Farla a Robinet C: Nilde Baracchi.
Il Yacht Misterioso C: Nilde Baracchi.

PART TWO: AMERICAN FILMS

AS DIRECTOR / ACTOR FOR JOKER:

A Day at Midland Beach (10/30/1915) Joker. Dist: Universal. 1 rl.
   Dir: Alan Curtis & Marcel Perez. C: Perez.

AS BUNGLES FOR VIM:
PD: Louis Burstein. D: Fernandea Perez. 1 reel.

Bungles' Rainy Day (2/10/1916) C: Perez, Elsie McLeod, Oliver
   Hardy

Bungles Enforces the Law (2/24/1916) C: Perez, Elsie McLeod, Oliver Hardy, Bobby Burns, Billy Ruge.

Bungles Elopement (3/9/1916) C: Perez, Elsie McLeod, Oliver Hardy.

Bungles Lands a Job (3/23/1916) C: Perez, Elsie McLeod, Oliver Hardy.

AS TWEEDLEDUM FOR EAGLE FILMS:
Dist: Unity Film Sales. PD: William J. Dunn. D: Marcel Perez.

Torpedoed by Cupid (6/19/1916) 1 rl. C: Perez, Nilde Baracchi, Rex Adams, Louise Carver, Tom Murray, Billy Slade. (a.k.a. *Tweedledum Torpedoed by Cupid*).

A Busy Night* (6/26/1916) 2 rls. C: Perez, Tom Murray. (a.k.a. *Tweedledum's Busy Night*) (LOC)

A Scrambled Honeymoon (7/3/1916) 2 rls. C: Perez. (a.k.a. *Tweedledum's Scrambled Honeymoon*).

Some Hero* (10/23/1916) 1 rl. C: Perez, Nilde Baracchi, Billy Slade, Jerry Jellman, Jim McGowan, Charles Sharp. (a.k.a. *He's Some Hero*). (MoMA)

A Lucky Tramp (11/6/1916) 1 rl. C: Perez, Nilde Baracchi, J. Melvin Andrews, Tom Murray.

Lend Me Your Wife* (11/13/1916) 2 rls. C: Perez, Nilde Baracchi, Louise Carver, J. Melvin Andrews, Tom Murray. (MoMA)

A Bath Tub Elopement *(11/20/1916) 1 rl. C: Perez, Nilde Baracchi, J. Melvin Andrews, Louise Carver, Tom Murray. (LOC)

A Short-Sighted Crime (11/27/1916) 2 rls. C: Perez.

Somewhere in Mexico (12/4/1916) 1 rl. C: Perez, Billy Slade.

The Burlesque Show* (12/11/1916) (listed in film journals as both one and two reels). C: Perez, Nilde Baracchi. (clips at LOC)

The Near-Sighted Auto-Pedist (12/1916) C: Perez, Nilde Baracchi, Billy Slade.

AS TWEDE-DAN FOR JESTER COMEDIES:
PD: William Steiner. 2 reels.

The Recruit (2/15/1918)C: Perez, Nilde Barachhi, Wilbert Shields.
His Golden Romance (3/15/1918) D: Courtlandt Van Dusen. 2 rls.
C: Perez.
All 'Fur' Her (4/15/1918) C: Perez.
The Wrong Flat (5/15/1918) C: Perez, Nilde Baracchi. (a.k.a. *In and Out*).
This is the Life (5/1918) C: Perez, Nilde Baracchi, Jane Wills, Thomas Regan. (a.k.a. *It's a Great Life*).
Oh! What a Day* (8/1/1918) D: William Seiter. 2 rls. C: Perez, Nilde Baracchi. (MoMA)
The Fly Ball (9/1/1918) D: William Seiter. 2 rls. C: Perez, Nilde Baracchi.
Ain't It So (10/1/1918) D: William Seiter. 2 rls. C: Perez.
Some Baby (11/1/1918) D: William Seiter. 2 rls. C: Perez.
Camouflage* (11/15/1918) D: William Seiter. 2 rls. C: Perez, Nilde Baracchi. (LOC)

SECOND SEASON AS TWEDE-DAN FOR JESTER COMEDIES:
PD: William Steiner. Dist: Territorial Sales Corp. D: Marcel Perez. 2 reels.

He Wins (1918) C: Perez, Nilde Baracchi.
In the Wild West (1919)C: Perez, Nilde Baracchi.
Peace and Riot (1919) C: Perez.
The Tenderfoot* (1919) C: Perez, Nilde Baracchi. (LOC)
A Mexican Mix-Up (1919) C: Perez, Nilde Baracchi.
The Wisest Fool (1919) C: Perez, James Harvey Holland.
Gee Whiz (1919) C: Perez.
Almost Married (1919) C: Perez.

Business Without Pleasure (1919) C: Perez.

Can You Beat It?* (1919) C: Perez, Dorothy Earle, Flo Bailey, Pierre Collosse, Amy Manning. (GEH)

The Frame Up (1919) C: Perez.

In the Swim (1919) C: Perez.

Chicken in Turkey (1919) C: Perez, Dorothy Earle, Pierre Collosse.

She-Me (1919) C: Perez.

You're Next* (1919) C: Perez, Dorothy Earle, Pierre Collosse, Billy Slade. (EYE, LOC)

AS TWEEDY FOR REELCRAFT:

Mirth Comedies. PD: Schiller Prods. Dist: Reelcraft. D: Marcel Perez. 2 reels.

Here He Is (5/16/1921) C: Perez.

Sweet Daddy* (1921) PH: Herman Obrock. C: Perez, Dorothy Earle, Wilna Hervey, Kit Guard. (EYE, LOC)

Chick, Chick (1921) C: Perez, Dorothy Earle.

Vacation (1921) C: Perez.

Speed (1921) C: Perez.

Wild * (1921) C: Perez, Dorothy Earle. (a.k.a. *Untamed*) (LOC)

The Knockout* (1921) C: Perez, Pierre Collosse, Martin Kinney. (clip at LOC)

Milk-Made (1921) C: Perez.

Moving (1921) C: Perez, Dorothy Earle, Pierre Collosse.

The Nut (1921) C: Perez.

Week End* (1921) C: Perez, Dorothy Earle, Pierre Collosse. (1st reel at EYE)

All In (1921) C: Perez.

All Around (1921) C: Perez.

Pinched* (1921) C: Perez, Dorothy Earle, Pierre Collosse. (NFA/BFI)

Why Worry (1921) C: Perez.

ALADDIN COMEDIES FOR REELCRAFT:
PD: Schiller Prods. Dist: Reelcraft.

*Shot** (1921) D: Marcel Perez. PH: Herman Obrock. 1 rl. C: Billy Moran, Dorothy Earle, Pierre Collosse, Perez (?). (GEH)

*Blowing Bubbles** (1921) D: Marcel Perez. PH: Herman Obrock. 1 rl. C: Billy Moran, Dorothy Earle.

Fireworks (1921) D: Marcel Perez. 1 rl. C: Billy Moran, Dorothy Earle.

TWEEDY COMEDIES FOR SANFORD PRODUCTIONS:
PD: Sanford Prods. D: Marcel Perez. 2 reels.

Fire — Fire (9/1/1922) C: Perez.
Take A Tip (10/1/1922) C: Perez.
Don't Monkey (11/1/1922) C: Perez.
Dog Gone It (12/1/1922) C: Perez.
Three O'Clock in the Morning (1/1/1923) C: Perez.
Friday 13th (2/1/1923) C: Perez.

FEATURES AS DIRECTOR:

*The Way Women Love** (1920) PD: Lyric Films/William Steiner Prod. Dist: Arrow Film Corp. D: Marcel Perez. PH: William Cooper. A: Herman Landon. 5 rls. C: Rubye De Remer, Edward Elkas, Walter D. Greene, Thomas Magrine, Walter Miller, Rose Mintz, Henry W. Pemberton. (LOC)

Luxury (1921) PD: Lyric Films/William Steiner Prod. Dist: Arrow Film Corp. D: Marcel Perez. 6 rls. C: Rubye De Remer, Fredrick Kalgren, Thomas Magrine, Rose Mintz, Henry W. Pemberton.

Unconquered Women (1922) PD: Pasha Film Corp. D: Marcel Perez. PH: William Cooper. 5 rls. C: Rubye De Remer, Fred C. Jones, Frankie Mann, Walter Miller, Nick Thompson.

*The Better Man Wins** (1922) PD: Sanford Prods. D: Marcel Perez & Frank S. Mattison. 6 rls. C: Pete Morrison, Dorothy Woods, Gene Crosby, E.L Van Sickle, Jack Walters, Tom Bay.

Duty First (1922) PD: Sanford Prods. D: Marcel Perez. 5 rls. C: Pete Morrison.

West vs. East (1922) PD: Sanford Prods. Dist: Arrow Film Corp. D: Marcel Perez. 5 rls. C: Pete Morrison, Dorothy Woods, Gene Crosby, Renee Danti, Beesie De Lich, Lorenz Gillette, Robert Gray.

Making Good (2/12/1923) PD: Sanford Prods. D: Marcel Perez. 5 rls. C: Pete Morrison, Eileen Sedgwick.

*Pioneers of the West** (1925) PD: William Mix Prods. D & A: Marcel Perez. PH: Elmer Dyer. 5 rls. C: Dick Carter, Dorothy Earle, Gene Crosby, Olin Francis, Bud Osborne. (This feature has an accepted release date of 6/1/19127, but I found a review in the Moving Picture World of 9/19/1925. The 1927 date may be a re-issue).

*Lash of the Law** (1926) PD: Goodwill Pictures, Inc. 5 rls. C: William Bailey, Alma Rayford, Marcel Perez, Dick La Reno, Bud Osborne, Roy Watson, Milton J. Fahrney. (No specific directorial credit is available for this film, but it was likely directed by Perez).

AS DIRECTOR FOR JOE ROCK PRODUCTIONS:
PD: Joe Rock/Standard Cinema Prods. Dist: FBO. D: Marcel Perez. 2 reels.

*Hold Tight** (11/15/1925) Blue Ribbon Comedy. C: Alice Ardell, Joe Rock, Bobby Dunn. (NFTS)

*A Peaceful Riot** (12/15/1925) Blue Ribbon Comedy. C: Alice Ardell, Slim Summerville, Max Asher, Leon Kent, Ethan Laidlaw, Harry Martel.

*Mummy Love** (1/10/1926) Blue Ribbon Comedy. C: Alice Ardell, Neely Edwards.(GEH, LOC)

*Alice Blues** (2/7/1926) Blue Ribbon Comedies. C: Alice Ardell, Sid
Smith, Martin Kinney, Harry Bowen, Joe Bonner, Harry Martel,
Leo Sulky. (EYE, MoMA)

The Hurricane (4/4/1926) Blue Ribbon Comedy. C: Alice Ardell.

*She's a Prince** (5/2/1926) Blue Ribbon Comedies. C: Alice Ardell,
Billy Franey, Billy Engle, Dorothy Vernon.

*The Vulgar Yachtsman** (11/15/1926) Standard Comedies. C:
Frank "Fatty" Alexander, Hilliard "Fatt" Karr, Bill "Kewpie"
Ross, Gale Henry, Lois Boyd. (EYE)

AS DIRECTOR & WRITER FOR UNIVERSAL:

Out All Night (9/4/1927) PD: Universal. D: William Seiter. A:
Gladys Lehman. Adapt: Harvey Thew & Marcel Perez. Titl: Tom
Reed. 6 rls. C: Reginald Denny, Marian Nixon, Wheeler Oakman,
Dorothy Earle, Dan Mason, Alfred Allen, Robert Seiter, Ben
Hendricks Jr., Billy Franey, Harry Tracy, Lionel Braham.

The Small Bachelor (11/6/1927) PD: Universal. D: William Seiter.
Sce: John Clymer. Titl: Walter Anthony. Adapt: Rex Taylor. Ad-
ditional material: Marcel Perez. Photo: Arthur Todd.   7 rls. C:
Barbara Kent, Andre Beranger, William Austin, Lucien Littlefield,
Carmelita Geraghty, Gertrude Astor, George Davis, Tom Dugan,
Vera Lewis, Ned Sparks.

His In-Laws (3/12/1928) PD: Universal. D: Marcel Perez. A: Oc-
tavious Roy Cohen. 2 rls. C: Charles Puffy.

FOR FURTHER RESEARCH:

Two of a Kind (1916) Jockey Comedy. Dist: Unicorn. C: Perez,
Babette Perez, Rex Adams, Tom Murray.

*Tweedledee and her Daughter** (ca 1916) The NFA/BFI has this
listed in their holdings. It could be an alternate title for any of his
American comedies, or from his elusive Jockey/Encore films.

SOCIETÀ ANONIMA AMBROSIO
Manifattura Cinematografica
—————— TORINO ——————

Brunner & C., Como

FABRE MARCEL

Ambrosio formal portrait of Perez during his Robinet years. *(Museo Nazionale del Cinema)*

Cine-Journal ad for the French release of *Robinet Innamorato di una Chanteuse* (*Robinet in Love with a Cabaret Singer*, 1911).

Cine-Journal ad for the French release of *Robinet edi Salvatori* (*Robinet and his Rescuer*, 1911).

Cine-Journal ad for the French release of *Il Pesce D'Aprile di Robinet* (*Robinet's April Fool Joke*, 1911).

"TWEEDLEDUM AND FRISCOT FIGHT A DUEL."
(Ambrosio.)

Tweedledum and Friscot, both in pursuit of the same attractive young lady, come into collison, angry words are exchanged,

followed by a challenge, and a duel is quickly fixed up. Swords are the weapons chosen, but unfortunately articles made of very inferior metal are chosen, and buckle up as soon as they are brought into play. Pistols are then procured, but a furious discharge sees the principals uninjured, though the seconds are one and all brought to the ground. Now recourse is had to heavier armaments, and each fighter stands by the side of a huge cannon, loaded to the muzzle with grapeshot. Still the result is the same—the new seconds are wiped out, but Tweedledum and Friscot are unscathed. So each enter a motor, and the two vehicles are driven full-tilt at each other. They are reduced to ruins, but the enemies are still intact, and in desperation take to an aeroplane each—which are driven together in mid-air, but only serve to precipitate the two combatants in the river together, where, finding themselves still unhurt, they embrace and swear eternal friendship.

Perez and Ernesto Vasar square off in this *Cinema News and Property Gazette* item for the British release of *Il Duello di Fricot* (*Robinet and Fricot Fight a Duel*, 1913).

"TWEEDLEDUM STUDIES MATHEMATICS." (*Ambrosio.*)

Tweedledum is deeply enamoured with the charming daughter of a prodigiously learned professor of mathematics, and when a note from the young lady informs him that her father is deeply preoccupied with a difficult problem, he loses no time in making a call. The professor is engaged in abstruse calculations on a blackboard, endeavouring to solve the sum expressed thus :— 1 + 1. Tweedledum, gallantly going to the rescue, makes the answer 3, but the professor is dissatisfied, and, leaving the young people alone, goes for a walk in order to revolve the problem. Every black surface which presents itself he employs as a blackboard—a door, the back of a wardrobe which a

workman is carrying, &c., being drawn into use, with results which are the reverse of pleasant for the professor when the owners discover what he is up to. Finally, he sets to work on the back of a carriage, and when it drives off follows at top speed, still figuring. The professor survives all kinds of collisions before the vehicle comes to a standstill, and then he gets the greatest shock of all, for the door opens and out steps his daughter and Tweedledum, whom he had imagined safe at home.

Cinema News and Property Gazette item for the British release of *Robinet Studia Matematia* (*Robinet Studies Mathematics*, 1913).

As Bungles for Vim, Perez adopted the Keystone style of facial hair, clearly visible in this ad for *Bungle's Rainy Day* (1916).

Besides the heavy eyebrows and mustache, Perez was supported by the Vim police force in *Bungles Enforces the Law* (1916).

Eagle exhibitor ad for the first group of Tweedledum comedies.

Fernando Pérez en sus distintas interpretaciones.

Another version of the photo from *A Busy Night* seen in a December 1916 promotional article in Spanish-language trade journal *Ciné-Mundial*. Note that for international markets he is referred to as Fernando Pérez.

Producer William Steiner pulled out all the publicity stops for the first season of Jester Comedies.

1918 Jester Comedy exhibitor ad.

Another 1918 Jester Comedy exhibitor ad.

British exhibitor ad from the trade magazine *The Bioscope. (The Cinema Museum London, UK)*

"Oh, What a Day!"

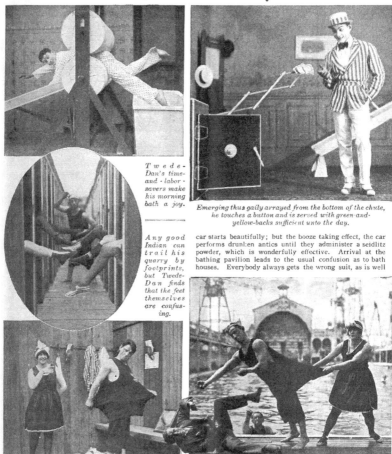

T w e d e - Dan's time- and - labor - savers make his morning bath a joy.

Emerging thus gaily arrayed from the bottom of the chute, he touches a button and is served with green-and-yellow-backs sufficient unto the day.

Any good Indian can trail his quarry by footprints, but Twede-Dan finds that the feet themselves are confusing.

car starts beautifully; but the booze taking effect, the car performs drunken antics until they administer a seidlitz powder, which is wonderfully effective. Arrival at the bathing pavilion leads to the usual confusion as to bath houses. Everybody always gets the wrong suit, as is well

He discovered that any bathing suit supplied at any beach can be relied on to make lean men look thinner, tall men more attenuated, and fat folks funnier.

The athlete with the ninety-pound wallop finds it is no good when Twede-Dan is in real form and negotiates a settlement of their differences.

Twede-Dan and his girl start for the beach in his new car. Seven miles from the nearest supply they run out of gas. They make this distance by man-power, to discover the price beyond their means; but prohibition has prevailed, and liquor is cheap. They fill the tank, and the

known. *Twede-Dan's* troubles are not lessened when his lady is overheard to explain that she will put her foot out, so he will know the right room. One slap-stick adventure follows another through gales of laughter, until the comedy ends with a surprise.

Film Fun magazine layout for the 1918 Jester *Oh, What a Day!*

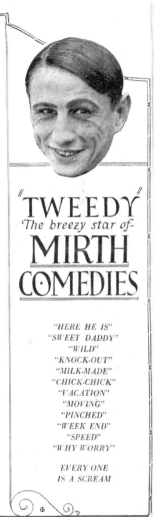
Perez was Reelcraft's biggest name during its final days.

Coming attraction slides for Tweedy Reelcraft comedies that were shown in cinemas. (*Cleveland Public Library Digital Gallery*)

Presents

TWEEDY

Released One-a-month   **Starting in May**

Supported by his own big company.   **Directed by Marcel Perez.**

In a New Series of Twelve Two-reel, High Class Comedies

First release—

FIRE! FIRE!

Now ready

Every comedy as complete a laughter knockout as
money, time and brains can produce.

SANFORD PRODUCTIONS

6046 and 6048 Sunset Boulevard   **Hollywood, California**

Exhibitor ad for Perez's last series of starring comedies.

JIMMY AUBREY

MAKES HIS BOW IN A NEW SERIES OF TWO REEL COMEDIES

JIMMY AUBREY
STAR
COMEDIES

STANDARD CINEMA CORPORATION *Releasing thru* **SELZNICK DISTRIBUTING CORPORATION**

Exhibitor ad for the Joe Rock-produced series of 1924 Jimmy Aubrey two-reelers.

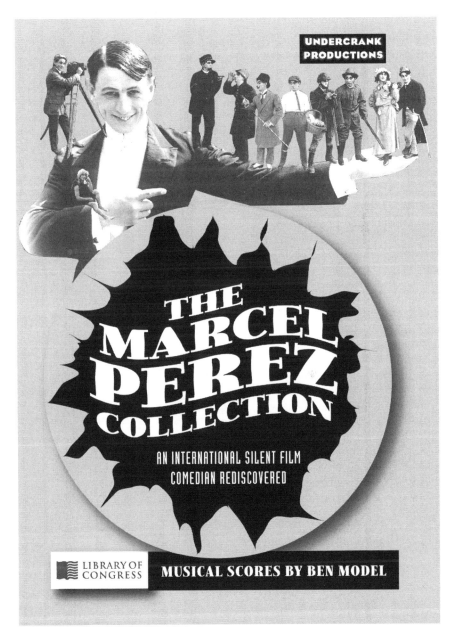

DVD box cover art for *The Marcel Perez Collection*, produced and released in 2015 by Undercrank Productions.

The Marcel Perez Collection DVD contains ten rare Marcel Perez comedy shorts, and marks the first time Perez' films have been available on home video. The DVD was produced and scored by Ben Model/Undercrank Productions, in association with the Library of Congress.

Italian Films: *Robinet in Love with a Singer* (1911), *Robinet's White Suit* (1911), *Mademoiselle Robinet* (1912), *Robinet is Too Much Loved By His Wife* (1912), and *Robinet is Jealous* (1914). These titles were preserved and transferred by EYE Filmmuseum (Netherlands), from archival 35mm prints in the Desmet Collection.

Film pioneer Jean Desmet (1875-1956) was the first major distributor and cinema owner in the Netherlands. The Desmet collection has been held by EYE Filmmuseum (Netherlands) since 1957, and includes many films from the early years of cinema that were once presumed lost. The collection includes 923 films on nitrate stock, nearly all originating from the period between 1907 and 1916. Most of the films are 'one-reelers', with a running time of about 15 minutes, and a large number of these films are unique copies (the only preserved copy in the world). The vast collection contains, among many other items, masterpieces by D.W. Griffith and Louis Feuillade, films with Asta Nielsen and Lyda Borelli, and productions from the film companies Pathé, Gaumont and Edison. The Desmet Collection at the EYE Filmmuseum Netherlands has been inscribed on the UNESCO Memory of the World Register.

American Films: *A Bathtub Elopement* (1916), *A Busy Night* (1916), *Camouflage* (1918), *You're Next* (1919), and *Sweet Daddy* (1921). These titles were preserved and transferred by the Library of Congress, from archival 35mm and 16mm prints.

The Library of Congress is home to more than 1.1 million film, television, and video items. With a collection ranging from motion pictures made in the 1890s to today's TV programs, the Library's holdings are an unparalleled record of American and international creativity in moving images.

Both the DVD, *The Marcel Perez Collection* and the book, *Marcel Perez: The International Mirth-Maker* were funded through Kickstarter by 154 fans and supporters.

The DVD is region-free and is available on Amazon.com. Visit www.undercrankproductions.com for more information about this and other releases.

ABOUT THE AUTHOR

STEVE MASSA is the author of *Lame Brains and Lunatics: The Good, The Bad, and The Forgotten of Silent Comedy*, and has organized comedy film programs for the Museum of Modern Art, the Library of Congress, the Smithsonian Institution, and the Pordenone Silent Film Festival. In addition to consulting with the EYE Filmmuseum, Netherlands and other archives, and writing for journals such as *Griffithiana*, he is a founding member of Silent Cinema Presentations which produces NYC's Silent Clowns Film Series. Steve has also contributed articles and commentary tracks to many DVD collections such as *The Forgotten Films of Roscoe "Fatty" Arbuckle*, *Harry Langdon: Lost and Found*, and Kino Lorber's *Buster Keaton: The Short Films Collection*, and Undercrank Productions' *The Mishaps of Musty Suffer*.

Made in the USA
Middletown, DE
29 December 2014